POWER OVER PAIN

100 Healing & Motivational Quotes

Amazon Best Selling Author

Tawana F. Sampson

POWER OVER PAIN

Author Tawana F. Sampson

Copyright © 2018 by 5Hearts Publishing Company.

Published by 5Hearts Publications, LLC.

All rights reserved. This book or any portion thereof may not be reproduced or used in any manner without the publisher's express written permission except for the use of brief quotations in a book review.

Disclaimer: This book is not intended to diagnose, treat, cure or prevent any disease.

Printed in the United States of America

First Edition, 2022

ISBN: 978-0-578-68900-5

POWER OVER PAIN

100 Healing & Motivational Quotes

Contents

Introduction 1
Thank You Note 2
Would You Do Me a Solid? 3
BACK STORY OF WHY I DECIDED TO WRITE THIS BOOK 4
QUOTES 5
A FEW SHORT POEMS FOR YOU 18
    Life 18
    Broken Wing 18
    Voices 19
Conclusion 20
Last Words of Encouragement 21

Introduction

Everyone in this walk of life goes through some type of pain in some form or fashion, but here's the rub. You have only two choices on how you deal with the pain. Either you can lay around and be like I used to be, crying, woe is me, repeating the same dysfunctional patterns of being stuck in a rut, or get up and do something about it. I hope this book will touch hearts around the world so this book is dedicated to the world.

Start practicing the knowledge inside this book; I believe three things will happen to you. First, your mind will get better.

You will be a better person, regardless of what happened to you.

Your life will be better.

Thank You Note

First, I want to thank my children, who walked with me through the fire and never gave up on me. You all wouldn't accept the person that was before you. Instead, you all pushed me with tough love. To all of my specialists, doctors, counselors, activists, and advocates, who played and still play an intricate part in my recovery, may God bless you good. Thanks to a special friend for handling me with TLC. You are so brilliant, and I'm most gracious to you. Finally, to everyone, who supports me online, I truly appreciate you.

Would You Do Me a Solid?

If you enjoyed *Power Over Pain,* would you mind taking a minute to write a review? Even a short review helps; it'd mean a lot to me. Also, if someone you care about is struggling, please send them a copy of this book.

Books can be purchased on Amazon.
Check out music to this book on Spotify, Amazon, YouTube, and other major platforms.
Artist: Kai Reads
Follow Kaireads FB
Check out Justice for Tawana FB

BACK STORY OF WHY I DECIDED TO WRITE THIS BOOK

On March 10, 2012, I suffered a severe brain injury, major depression, severe PSTD, and severe anxiety. My injuries were so painful to the point that I came up with a plan to commit suicide. Why? I didn't have any medical insurance.

Hospitals kept referring me to neurologists, and neurologists referred me right back to the hospitals. They bounced me back and forth with no relief like a ping pong ball. Eventually, I was admitted to the psych ward. LIFE was OVER! At least, that's what I thought. I thought no one could help me, so what was I to do other than clock of this life? For almost four years, I took eight different medications, putting together concoctions, and thinking, this is **NOW MY LIFE**.

But one sweet day, I got tired of the pain that seemed to have power over me and decided to take **POWER OVER PAIN**. This is what I've learned in the process.

QUOTES

1. Wait, the storm out. Storms are temporary disruptions.

2. Be a fountain, not a drain. Fountains flow while drains empty.

3. Yesterday, I was devastated. Yet, today, I am still going.

4. Every time you think you will break down, you get stronger.

5. Life is like having a baby. Keep pushing.

6. Worry less by distracting your mind.

7. Your pain is birthing something inside of you. Live and let go.

8. To be more than the average, you have to become more than the average.

9. Search for answers until there aren't any options left.

10. Press through the pain. Do what you have to do.

11. Don't wait for something to happen. Make it happen.

12. Be grateful for the smallest things in life; the larger things will attract to you.

13. Nobody can keep you from your destiny but you.

14. Life is like a chess game, and we all play. So study your next move carefully because the game will be played whether you want to.

15. Find one thing to be happy about. A day doesn't go by without one thing to be happy about.

16. Rain falls, but it always dry.

17. Trauma can never be forgotten, but it can be forgiven. Set yourself free.

18. Smile today, if only for a good memory.

19. You are never alone because you always have you.

20. Your dreams and goals might be on hold, but they are not inevitable.

21. When you use your pain to push you forward, it will always give you strength.

22. Speak good words into your life and watch them manifest.

23. Once you get past the pity party, it's time to party.

24. Your testimony could help someone else.

25. All of us have a champion inside of us.

26. Who can advocate for you better than yourself? No one. You know your story better than anyone else.

27. Celebrate the uncelebrateable.

28. Sometimes, pain chooses us without our consent.

29. Giving up is not an option. So what are you going to do?

30. If you can't go through the door of opportunity, climb through a window.

31. A beautiful thing can be born out of your pain if you allow it.

32. You and no one else are in control of you.

33. If you can't take care of yourself, then you cannot take care of anyone else. Be well.

34. Inhale positivity. Exhale negativity. Repeat until relieved.

35. The possibilities are endless in our lives. Believe that.

36. Sometimes your mind needs a break from the hustle and bustle. Quiet times equal a calm mind.

37. People may look at you like you haven't changed. But the funny thing is they haven't changed because they would see you differently if they did. Keep Going.

38. You are responsible for your happiness.

39. Everyone is born with a gift or talent. Seek, and ye shall find.

40. Therapy is a way to dump off all your problems. Empty yourself to the fullest and leave fulfilled.

41. If you aren't satisfied with a therapist, find another one until you find your match. It's like a relationship, looking for a mate. This could be why many people quit and think therapy doesn't work. Stay Patient. Don't stop searching.

42. It's OK to mess up, but don't waddle. Get back up.

43. Don't talk about it. Be about it. Remember, actions speak louder than words.

44. You are a survivor. Your battle scars prove it.

45. When people don't understand you, you do, and that's all that matters.

46. Life has a reset button. Anyone can start over at any time.

47. Through recovery, you may have several counselors. However, you will know in your heart when it's time to find another.

48. Think you're too old to go after your dreams? Well, you're not.

49. You have to understand to understand.

50. Give it your all when you don't have anything else to give.

51. Winning is not always about being in first place. Let somebody else shine.

52. If you ring the doorbell of opportunities enough times, one of the doors will open.

53. Life will throw curve balls, so keep on your glove.

54. When you think things are working against you, maybe they are not. But, on the other hand, maybe things are working as they should.

55. Be ready for change. Change is always happening, whether good or bad.

56. Make ways, not excuses.

57. Stay in the fight. When you can't find your way, that is the time to fight harder.

58. Gratitude is the right attitude.

59. Everybody has a story, but not everyone will be brave enough to tell it.

60. Kind deeds are planting good seeds in the garden called life.

61. Open the blinds in your house and let the light shine through. Doing this can change your mood.

62. Positive and negative energy surrounds everyone. Practice deciphering the difference.

63. Wake up expecting a good day every day.

64. Look fear dead in the eyes and say, "I'm not scared of you! You ole (F)alse (E)xpectation (A)lways (R)oaming!

65. Stop chasing your dreams; Catch them.

66. Start now, even if you don't have all the tools.

67. When you stop hanging around negative people, you will attract positive people.

68. Ask yourself if the people you are around are elevating you to a higher level or bringing you down.

69. Learn to enjoy the quietness. It's pretty fascinating.

70. Sing to those who are negative in your life. Na, Na, Na, Na, Na, hey, hey…Goodbye.

71. The Law of Attraction is working against you or for you. The fascinating thing about it is you get to choose which one.

72. Reprogramming your mind takes work.

73. Become a data mine specialist. The internet has answers. It's an information brain.

74. Unsubscribe to things, people, and conversations that no longer serve you.

75. Ask, believe, and receive. Asking and receiving are easy. It's the believing part that challenges us.

76. Quickly put your negative emotions in check and think good thoughts.

77. Expect good things to happen, and they will.

78. L.I.M.E.S.-Rearrange the letters. SMILE

79. Faith is a strong belief in something. It is acceptance with certainty, confidence, and conviction.

80. Slow doesn't mean no. No means **N**ext **O**pportunity.

81. You might fall, but you don't have to stay down.

82. Waiting on an answer that can change your life may have you on pins and needles. While waiting, find some material and sew yourself together another plan.

83. One idea can turn into many. Build.

84. Forgive yourself for past mistakes that you made. Why are you still holding on to them?

85. Focus on what you are doing and not what others are doing.

86. Sometimes, we are sent to the beginning just to start again to do it better.

87. When you focus on helping people instead of what you can get out of it. You are Winning!

88. Everyone is valuable.

89. The best gift in life is living.

90. We don't pursue our goals and dreams because we think we lack the knowledge to succeed. However, we are capable of doing more than we think we are.

91. When people say you can't. Say, **I CAN**! When people say you are nobody. Say, **I AM SOMEBODY**! When people say you are not going anywhere. Say, **I'M GOING SOMEWHERE!**

92. Take up your bed and walk or keep lying down. Are you getting up or what?

93. Realize this. Some people will try to deter or make you feel bad whenever you are changing for the better. You are coming out of a cocoon—Fly, butterfly. Fly.

94. Are you living in a gloomy atmosphere where you cannot escape? Then, build yourself inside, and know you will be free from it someday. It's just a matter of time.

95. Meditate, pray, think of a good memory or play some music to cross back to the positive field.

96. The atmosphere gives you back what you are giving to it. It's called the Boomerang Effect.

97. Always love yourself.

98. Pay it forward sometimes. It is better to give than to receive.

99. Stop being a victim. Be Victorious

100. Be your best cheerleader

A FEW SHORT POEMS FOR YOU

Life

The sun is beaming on the window pane

It wants to know how you are feeling today

Without one single trace of rain

The sun is saying everything is going to be OK

Life wants you to be happy

Life wants to see you smile

Life is so beautiful

Life gone be alright, Chile

Broken Wing

An angel broke its wing

Trying to rescue a soul

The soul is the one that broke the angel's wing

The angel asked the soul, "Why are you fighting against me?"

The soul answered, "I don't want you to save me. I'm in too much pain. Too much, that I can no longer bear."

"Look at my wing that you broke and I'm still fighting for you. I will fight until the end to save your soul, if I have to lose my other wing."

The soul looked in the mirror.

"I don't want you to lose both wings. I don't want you to die." The angel's broken wing healed.

Voices

Voices from my past won't leave me alone.

Taunting me and haunting me like nobody's business

Today, I'm choosing to stop listening

It hasn't got me anywhere, anyways

Serving as a distraction

Oh my

I've been giving those voices a reaction

That is why they stuck around all these years

They've been feeding off my tears and fears of letting go

Giving them the strength to grow

But not anymore

Voices from my past won't leave me alone

Taunting me and haunting me like nobody's business

Today, I'm choosing to stop listening

It hasn't got me anywhere, anyways

Conclusion

Who told you the world owes you something? I'm sure the world owes you something, said no one ever. So don't take this personal. Then again, please do, but seriously though. I'm hoping you will take all the pain, hurt, resentment, bitterness, unforgiveness, trauma, and any emotion tied to the negativity you're still harboring in your life and say, junk it. I refuse to carry these weights any longer and reference back to this book whenever you feel the need to take Power Over Pain.

Last Words of Encouragement

I challenge you to use the blank pages at the end of this book to write down some of your goals.

It could be starting a business, music, writing a book, buying a home, or even taking a vacation.

You might say, I don't have everything I need to do this or that; however, everything you need is already inside you—peace, love, and light.

Blessings,
Kai Reads (Tawana Sampson)

Made in the USA
Columbia, SC
14 November 2022